life

.

life

A User's Manual

EDITED BY JOHN MILLER

WITH ELIZA FINKELSTEIN

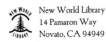 New World Library
14 Pamaron Way
Novato, CA 94949

Cover and text design: Big Fish

Library of Congress Cataloging-in-Publication Data

Life : a user's manual / edited by John Miller, with Eliza Finklestein.
p. cm.
ISBN 1-57731-067-5 (hardcover : alk. paper)
1. Literature—collections. 2. Conduct of life—Literary collections.
I. Miller, John, 1959—   . II. Finklestein, Eliza
PN6014.L54 1998   98-3733
808.8'038—dc21   CIP

First printing, May 1998
ISBN 1-57731-067-5
Printed in the U.S.A. on acid-free paper
Distributed to the trade by Publishers Group West
10 9 8 7 6 5 4 3 2

FOR JIM KEITH

"Contradiction is perhaps the subtlest of all spiritual forces."

—ALBERT CAMUS

Contents

search

"The quest is one and the same . . . We are all drawn toward the same craters of the spirit — to know what we are, and what we are for, to know our purpose. . . ."

—SAUL BELLOW

The Moviegoer

WALKER PERCY

What is the nature of the search? you ask.

Really it is very simple, at least for a fellow like me; so simple that it is easily overlooked.

The search is what anyone would undertake if he were not sunk in the everydayness of his own life. This morning, for example, I felt as if I had come to myself on a strange island. And what does such a castaway do? Why, he pokes around the neighborhood and he doesn't miss a trick.

To become aware of the possibility of the search is to be onto something. Not to be onto something is to be in despair.

The movies are onto the search, but they screw it up. The search always ends in despair. They like to show a fellow coming to himself in a strange place — but what does he do? He takes up with the local librarian, sets about proving to the local children what a nice fellow he is, and settles down with a vengeance. In two weeks' time he is so sunk in everydayness that he might just as well be dead.

What do you seek — God? you ask with a smile.

I hesitate to answer, since all other Americans have settled the matter for themselves and to give such an answer would amount to setting myself a goal which everyone else has reached — and therefore raising a question in which no one has the slightest interest. Who wants to be dead last among one hundred and eighty million Americans? For, as everyone knows, the polls report that 98 percent of Americans believe in God and the remaining 2 percent are atheists and agnostics — which leaves not a single percentage point for a seeker. For myself, I enjoy answering polls as much as anyone and take pleasure in giving intelligent replies to all questions.

Truthfully, it is the fear of exposing my own ignorance which constrains me from mentioning the object of my own search. For, to begin with, I cannot even answer this, the simplest and most basic of all questions: Am I, in my search, a hundred miles ahead of my fellow Americans or a hundred miles behind them? This is to say: Have 98 percent of Americans already found what I seek or are they so sunk in everydayness that not even the possibility of a search has occurred to them?

On my honor, I do not know the answer.

A Few Pounds of Dreams

DIANE ACKERMAN

After all, mind is such an odd predicament for matter to get into. I often marvel how something like hydrogen, the simplest atom, forged in some early chaos of the universe, could lead to us and the gorgeous fever we call consciousness. If a mind is just a few pounds of blood, dream and electric, how does it manage to contemplate itself, worry about its soul, do time-and-motion studies, admire the shy hooves of a goat, know that it will die, enjoy all the grand and lesser mayhems of the heart? What is mind, that one can be *out of one's*? How can a neuron feel compassion? What is a self? Why did automatic, hand-me-down mammals like our ancestors somehow evolve brains with the ability to consider, imagine, project, compare, abstract, think of the future? If our experience of mind is really just the simmering of an easily alterable chemical stew, then what does it mean to *know* something, to *want* something to *be*.

Religion

ZORA NEALE HURSTON

You wouldn't think that a person who was born with God in the house would ever have any questions to ask on the subject.

But as early as I can remember, I was questing and seeking. It was not that I did not hear. I tumbled right into the Missionary Baptist Church when I was born. I saw the preachers and the pulpits, the people and the pews. Both at home and from the pulpit, I heard my father, known to thousands as "Reverend Jno" (an abbreviation for John) explain all about God's habits, His heaven, His ways, and Means. Everything was known and settled.

From the pews I heard a ready acceptance of all that Papa said. Feet beneath the pews beat out a rhythm as he pictured the scenery of heaven. Heads nodded with conviction in time to Papa's words. Tense snatches of tune broke out and some shouted until they fell into a trance at the recognition of what they heard from the pulpit. Come "love feast," some of the congregation told of getting close enough to peep into God's sitting room windows. Some went further. They had been inside the place and looked all around. They spoke of sights and scenes around God's throne.

That should have been enough for me. But somehow it left a lack in my mind. They should have looked and acted differently from other people after experiences like that. But these people looked and acted like everybody else — or so it seemed to me. They ploughed, chopped wood, went possum-hunting, washed clothes, raked up back-yards and cooked collard greens like anybody else. No more ornaments and nothing. It mystified me. There were so many things they neglected to look after while they were right there in the presence of All-Power. I made up my mind to do better than that if ever I made the trip.

I wanted to know, for instance, why didn't God make grown babies instead of those little measly things that messed up didies and cried all the time? What was the sense of making babies with no teeth? He knew that they had to have teeth, didn't He? So why not give babies their teeth in the beginning instead of hiding the toothless things in hollow stumps and logs for grannies and doctors to find and give to people? He could see all the trouble people had with babies, rubbing their gums and putting wood-lice around their necks to get them to cut teeth. Why did God hate for children to play on Sundays? If Christ, God's son, hated to die, and God hated for Him to die and have everybody grieving over it ever since, why did He have to do it? Why did people die anyway?

It was explained to me that Christ died to save the world from sin and then too, so that folks did not have to die anymore. That was a simple, clear-cut explanation. But then I heard my father and other preachers accusing people of sin. They went so far as to say that people were so prone to sin, that they sinned with every breath they drew. You couldn't even breathe without sinning!

How could that happen if we had already been saved from it? So far as the dying part was concerned, I saw enough funerals to know that somebody was dying. It seemed to me that somebody had been fooled and I so stated to my father and two of his colleagues. When they got through with me, I knew better than to say that out loud again, but their shocked and angry tirades did nothing for my bewilderment. My head was full of misty fumes of doubt.

Neither could I understand the passionate declarations of love for a being that nobody could see. Your family, your puppy and the new bull-calf, yes. But a spirit away off who found fault with everybody all the time, that was more than I could fathom. When I was asked if I loved God, I always said yes because I knew that that was the thing I was supposed to say. It was a guilty secret with me for a long time. I did not dare ask even my chums if they meant it when they said they loved God with all their souls and minds and hearts, and would be glad to die if He wanted them to. Maybe they had found out how to do it, and I was afraid of what they might say if they found out I hadn't. Maybe they wouldn't even play with me anymore.

But certain things have seemed to me to be true as I heard the tongues of those who had speech, and listened at the lips of books. It seems to me to be true that heavens are placed in the sky because it is the unreachable. The unreachable and therefore the unknowable always seem divine — hence, religion. People need religion because the great masses fear life and its consequences. Its responsibilities weigh heavy. Feeling a weakness in the face of great forces, men seek an alliance with omnipotence to bolster up their feeling of weakness, even though the omnipotence they rely upon is a creature of their own minds. It gives them a feeling of security. Strong, self-determining men are notorious for their lack of reverence. Constantine, having converted millions to Christianity by the sword, himself refused the consolation of Christ until his last hour. Some say not even then.

As for me, I do not pretend to read God's mind. If He has a plan of the Universe worked out to the smallest detail, it would be folly for me to presume to get down on my knees and attempt to revise it. That, to me, seems the highest form of sacrilege. So I do not pray. I accept the means at my disposal for working out my destiny. It seems to me that I have been given a mind and will-power for that very purpose. I do not expect God to single me out and grant me advantages over my fellow men. Prayer is for those who need it. Prayer seems to me a cry of weakness, and an attempt to avoid, by trickery, the rules of the game as laid down. I do not choose to admit weakness. I accept the challenge of responsibility. Life, as it is, does not frighten me, since I have made my peace with the universe as I find it, and bow to its laws. The ever-sleepless sea in its bed, crying out "how long?" to Time; million-formed and never motionless flame; the contemplation of these two aspects alone, affords me sufficient food for ten spans of my expected lifetime. It seems to me that organized creeds are collections of words around a wish. I feel no need for such. However, I would not, by word or deed, attempt to deprive another of the consolation it affords. It is simply not for me.

Somebody else may have my rapturous glance at the archangels. The springing of the yellow line of morning out of the misty deep dawn, is glory enough for me. I know that nothing is destructible; things merely change forms. When the consciousness we know as life ceases, I know that I shall still be part and parcel of the world. I was a part before the sun rolled into shape and burst forth in the glory of change. I was, when the earth was hurled out from its fiery rim. I shall return with the earth to Father Sun, and still exist in substance when the sun has lost its fire, and disintegrated in infinity to perhaps become part of the whirling rubble in space. Why fear? The stuff of my being is matter, ever changing, ever moving, but never lost; so what need of denominations and creeds to deny myself the comfort of all my fellow men? The wide belt of the universe has no need for finger-rings. I am one with the infinite and need no other assurance.

Ageless Body, Timeless Mind

DEEPAK CHOPRA

The ultimate boundary to human life is death, and for thousands of years we have tried to travel beyond that boundary. Despite the obvious mortality of our bodies, moments arise when the clear perception of immortality shines through. The poet Tennyson wrote of experiences he had in his youth when his individual self "seemed to dissolve and melt away into boundless being." This radical shift out of ordinary experience "was not a confused state," he recalled, "but the clearest of the clear, the surest of the sure, utterly beyond words — when death was an almost laughable impossibility."

Because they are totally subjective, such immortal feelings do not fit in to the worldview of science, and therefore we tend to label them religious. But thousands of people have been privileged to catch glimpses of the reality that encloses space and time like a vast multidimensional bubble. Some people seem to have contacted this timeless realm through near-death experiences, but it is also accessible in everyday life.

Peeking through the mask of matter "we have a certain feeling, a certain longing that we can't quite put into words. It's a striving . . . a wish for something greater or higher in ourselves." With these words the philosopher Jacob Needleman pointed to what he called "our second world," which anyone can access under special conditions.

Our first world, Needleman wrote, is "the world we live in every day, this world of action and activity and doing," ruled by everyday thoughts and emotions. But like flashes of spiritual lightning, there are moments when the second world makes itself known, full of peace and joy and a clear, unforgettable sense of who we really are — "vivid moments of being present in oneself," Needleman called them. If the second world is inside us, so is the first, because ultimately there is nothing verifiably "out there." Everything to be seen, felt, and touched in the world is knowable only as firings of neuron signals inside our brains. It all happens in here.

Who you are depends on what world you see yourself living in. Because it is ruled by change, the first world contains sickness, aging, and death as inevitable parts of the scenery; in the second world, where there is only pure being, these are totally absent. Therefore, finding this world within ourselves and experiencing it, even for a moment, could have a profound effect on the process of sickness and aging, if not death itself.

This possibility has always been accepted as fact in the East. In India and China, some spiritual masters are believed to have lived hundreds of years as a result of achieving a state of timeless awareness. This is considered one of the options open to a spirit who has attained Moksha, or liberation, although not every master takes the option of extending his life span. In the West, such powers are viewed with extreme skepticism. But the new paradigm assures us that there is a level of Nature where time dissolves, or, to turn it around, where time is created.

This level is extremely enigmatic, even by quantum standards, since it existed before the creation of space and time. The rational mind can't conceive of such a state, because to say that something existed before time began is a contradiction in logic. Yet the ancient sages believed that direct knowledge of timeless reality is possible. Every generation has affirmed that assertion. Einstein himself experienced episodes of complete liberation from space-time boundaries: "At such moments one imagines that one stands on some spot of a small planet gazing in amazement at the cold and yet profoundly moving beauty of the eternal, the unfathomable. Life and death flow into one, and there is neither evolution nor eternity, only Being."

It has taken three generations for the new paradigm to show us that Being is a very real state, existing beyond change and death, a place where the laws of Nature that govern change are overturned. Death is ultimately just another transformation, from one configuration of matter and energy to another. But unless you stand outside the arena of change, death represents an end point, an extinction. To escape death ultimately means escaping the worldview that gives death its terrible sense of closure and finality.

"I'm very afraid of death," an Indian disciple once confessed to his guru. "It's haunted me since I was a child. Why was I born? What will happen to me when I die?"

The guru considered the matter thoughtfully and said, "Why do you think you were born?"

"I don't understand your question," the disciple stammered.

"Why do you think you were born?" the guru repeated. "Isn't it just something your parents told you that you took for granted? Did you actually have the experience of being born, of coming into existence from a state of nonexistence, or didn't it happen that one day in childhood you asked where you came from, and your parents told you that you were born? Because you accepted their answer, the idea of death frightens you. But rest assured, you cannot have birth without death. They are two poles of the same concept. Perhaps you have always been alive and always will be. But in accepting your parents' system of belief, you entered into an agreement to fear death, because you think of it as an ending. Perhaps there is no ending — that is the possibility most worth exploring."

Naturally the disciple was shocked, because, like the rest of us, he didn't see death as a belief he had agreed to. What the guru was pointing out is that birth and death are space-time events but existence isn't. If we look inside us, we find a faint but certain memory that we have always been around. To put it another way, no one remembers *not* existing. The fact that such metaphysical issues arise shows how unique humans are. For us, death isn't just a brute fact but a mystery, and it must be unraveled before the mystery of aging — the process that leads to death — can be solved. The very deepest questions about who we are and what life means are wrapped up in the nature of existence.

When the spell of mortality is broken, you can release the fear that gives death its power. Fear of death reaches much further into our lives than our conscious minds are willing to concede. As David Viscott wrote, "When you say you fear death you are really saying that you fear you have not lived your true life. This fear cloaks the world in silent suffering." Yet by seeing through the fear you can turn it into a positive force. "Let your fear of death motivate you to examine your true worth and to have a dream for your own life," Viscott encouraged. "Let it help you value the moment, act on it, and live in it."

I want to go even further and suggest that when you see yourself in terms of timeless, deathless Being, every cell awakens to a new existence. True immortality can be experienced here and now, in this living body. It comes about when you draw the infusion of Being into everything you think and do. This is the experience of timeless mind and ageless body that the new paradigm has been preparing us for.

When All You've Ever Wanted Isn't Enough

HAROLD KUSHNER

If logic tells us that life is a meaningless accident, says Ecclesiastes at the end of his journey, don't give up on life. Give up on logic. Listen to that voice inside you which prompted you to ask the question in the first place. If logic tells you that in the long run, nothing makes a difference because we all die and disappear, then *don't live in the long run.* Instead of brooding over the fact that nothing lasts, accept that as one of the truths of life, and learn to find meaning and purpose in the transitory, in the joys that fade. Learn to savor the moment, even if it does not last forever. In fact, learn to savor it *because* it is only a moment and will not last. Moments of our lives can be eternal without being everlasting. Can you stop and close your eyes and remember something that happened for only a moment or two many years ago? It may have been a view of a spectacular landscape, or a conversation that made you feel loved and appreciated. In a sense it did not last very long at all, but in another sense it has lasted all those years and is still going on. That is the only kind of eternity this world grants us. Can you close your eyes and conjure up the memory of someone who is now dead but once meant a lot to you? Can you, in your mind, hear her voice and feel her touch? There is proof that a person, by learning how to live, can cheat death and live on beyond her allotted years.

When we stop searching for the Great Answer, the Immortal Deed which will give our lives ongoing meaning, and instead concentrate on filling our individual days with moments that gratify us, then we will find the only possible answer to the question, What is life about? It is not about writing great books, amassing great wealth, achieving great power. It is about loving and being loved. It is about enjoying your food and sitting in the sun rather than rushing through lunch and hurrying back to the office. It is about savoring the beauty of the moments that don't last, the sunsets, the leaves turning color, the rare moments of true human communication. It is about savoring them rather than missing out on them because we are so busy and they will not hold still until we get around to them. The author of Ecclesiastes spent most of his life looking for the Grand Solution, the Big Answer to the

Big Question, only to learn after wasting many years that try-ing to find one Big Answer to the problem of living is like trying to eat one Big Meal so that you will never have to worry about being hungry again. There is no Answer, but there are answers: love and the joy of working, and the simple pleasures of food and fresh clothes, the little things that tend to get lost and trampled in the search for the Grand Solution to the Problem of Life and emerge, like the proverbial bluebird of happiness, only when we have stopped searching. When we come to that stage in our lives when we are less able to accomplish but more able to enjoy, we will have attained the wisdom that Ecclesiastes finally found after so many false starts and disappointments.

Corita Kent, the former nun turned graphic artist, says in one of her posters, "Life is a series of moments/to live each one is to succeed." We misunderstand what it really means to be alive if we think that we can solve the problem of living once and for all by acquiring wealth, acquiring an education, acquiring a suitable husband or wife. We never solve the problem of living once and for all. We can only deal with it day by day, a constant struggle to fill each day with one day's worth of meaning. This, ultimately, is Ecclesiastes' insight and advice to us. Our author looked in vain for the key to the meaning of life. Try as he might, he could never find it. But despite his repeated failures, he could not bring himself to conclude that life was meaningless. He saw and felt the futility, the injustice of so much that happens to us on earth. But at the same time, he sensed that life, however muddled and frustrating, was too sacred, too special, too full of possibilities to be meaningless, even though he could never find that meaning. At last, he found it not in a few great deeds but in thousands of little ones.

love

"Cultivate a boundless heart
toward all beings . . ."

—SUTTA NIPATA

The Silent Life Giver

FRIDA KAHLO

the silent life giver
of worlds, what is most
important is the nonillusion.
morning breaks, the
friendly reds, the big
blues, hands full of leaves,
noisy birds, fingers
in the hair, pigeons' nests
a rare understanding of
human struggle simplicity
of the senseless song
the folly of the wind in my
heart = don't let them rhyme girl
= sweet xocolatl [chocolate] of ancient
Mexico, storm in the
blood that comes in through the
mouth — convulsion, omen,

laughter and sheer teeth needles
of pearl, for some gift on a seventh of July, I
ask for it, I get it, I sing,
sang. I'll sing from
now on our magic — love.

Markings

DAG HAMMARSKJÖLD

The "great" commitment all too easily obscures the "little" one. But without the humility and warmth which you have to develop in your relations to the few with whom you are personally involved, you will never be able to do anything for the many. Without them, you will live in a world of abstractions, where your solipsism, your greed for power, and your death-wish lack the one opponent which is stronger than they — love. Love, which is without an object, the outflowing of a power released by self-surrender, but which would remain a sublime sort of superhuman self-assertion, powerless against the negative forces within you, if it were not tamed by the yoke of human intimacy and warmed by its tenderness. It is better for the health of the soul to make one man good than "to sacrifice oneself for mankind." For a mature man, these are not alternatives, but two aspects of self-realization, which mutually support each other, both being the outcome of one and the same choice.

Love

MARTIN LUTHER KING, JR.

You've got to love the white man. God knows he needs our love. Now let me say to you that I'm not talking about emotional warmth when I talk about love. I'm not talking about sentimental emotion. But let me tell you what I mean when I say love. Now there are three words in the language of love. And I'm not trying to talk over anybody's head. I'm trying to get at a basic truth here.

There is a word *eros*. A Greek word. That word means love. But it means a sort of romantic love. You know this is the kind of love that you have for your mate. Romantic love is inevitably a little selfish. You love your lover because there is something about your lover that *moves* you.

That's eros. It may be the way he or she talks or the way he or she walks or the personality or the physical beauty or the intellectual power — or any of that — but it's always based on that there's something that attracts *you*. That's eros.

Now the Greek language has another word. *Philia.*

Which is a sort of intimate affection between personal friends. These are the people that you like. It's a reciprocal love. You love because you are loved. You love the people that you like. People that you like to sit down at the table and eat dinner with. People that you dial the phone and talk to. The people that you go out with. This is friendship.

Then the Greek language comes out with another word, my friends, and I don't want you to forget it. The word is *agape.* Agape is more than romantic love. Agape is more than friendship. Agape is understanding. It is creative and redeeming good will toward all men. It is the love of God operating in the human heart. It is the overflowing love which seeks nothing in return. And when you rise to love on this level, you love people who don't move you. You love those that you don't like. You love those whose ways are distasteful to you. You love every man because God loves him.

Wisdom of the Desert

THOMAS MERTON

All through the [Writings of the Desert Fathers] we find a repeated insistence on the primacy of love over everything else in the spiritual life: over knowledge, gnosis, asceticism, contemplation, solitude, prayer. Love in fact *is* the spiritual life, and without it all the other exercises of the spirit, however lofty, are emptied of content and become mere illusions. The more lofty they are, the more dangerous the illusion.

Love, of course, means something much more than mere sentiment, much more than token favours and perfunctory almsdeeds. Love means an interior and spiritual identification with one's brother, so that he is not regarded as an "object" to "which" one "does good." The fact is that good done to another as to an object is of little or no spiritual value. Love takes one's neighbour as one's other self, and loves him with all the immense humility and discretion and reserve and reverence without which no one can presume to enter into the sanctuary of another's subjectivity. From such love all authoritarian brutality, all exploitation, domineering and condescension must necessarily be absent. The saints of the desert were enemies of every subtle or gross expedient by which "the spiritual man" contrives to bully those he thinks inferior to himself, thus gratifying his own ego. They had renounced everything that savoured of punishment and revenge, however hidden it might be.

The Seventh Letter

RAINER MARIA RILKE

To love is also good, for love is difficult. For one human being to love another is perhaps the most difficult task of all, the epitome, the ultimate test. It is that striving for which all other striving is merely preparation. For that reason young people — who are beginners in everything — cannot yet love; they do not know how to love. They must learn it. With their whole being, with all strengths enveloping their lonely, disquieted heart, they must learn to love — even while their heartbeat is quickening. However, the process of learning always involves time set aside for solitude. Thus to love constantly and far into a lifespan is indeed aloneness, heightened and deepened aloneness for one who loves.

Love does not at first have anything to do with arousal, surrender, and uniting with another being — for what union can be built upon uncertainty, immaturity, and lack of coherence? Love is a high inducement for individuals to ripen, to strive to mature in the inner self, to manifest maturity in the outer world, to become that manifestation for the sake of another. This is a great, demanding task; it calls one to expand one's horizon greatly. Only in this sense, as the task to work on themselves, day and night, and to listen, ought young people use the love granted them. Opening one's self, and surrendering, and every kind of communion is not for them yet; they must for a very, very long time gather and harbor experience. It is the final goal, perhaps one which human beings as yet hardly ever seek to attain.

Young people often err, and that intensely so, in this way, since it is their nature to be impatient: They throw themselves at each other when loves comes upon them. They fragment themselves, just as they are, in all of their disarray and confusion. But what is to follow? What should fate do if this takes root, this heap of half-broken things that they call togetherness and that they would like to call their happiness?

What of their future? Everyone loses himself for the sake of the other and loses the other and many others that would yet have wished to come. They lose perspective and limit opportunities. They exchange the softly advancing and retreating of gentle premonitions of the spirit for an unfruitful restlessness. Nothing can come of it; nothing, that is, but disappointment, poverty, and escape into one of the many conventions that have been put up in great numbers, like public shelters, on this most dangerous road. No area of human experience is provided with as many conventions as this one: there are flotation devices of the most unusual sort; there are boats and life belts. Society has known how to create every kind of refuge conceivable. Since it is inclined to perceive love life as entertainment, it needs to display it as easily available, inexpensive, safe, and reliable, just like common public entertainment.

It is true that many young people who do not love rightly, who simply surrender themselves and leave no room for aloneness, experience the depressing feeling of failure. They would, in their own personal way, like to turn the condition in which they find themselves into something meaningful and fruitful. Their nature tells them that questions of love can be solved even less easily than everything else usually considered important, and certainly not publicly or by this or that agreement. Questions of love are personal, intimate questions, from one person to another, that in every case require a new, a special, and an *exclusively* personal answer. But then, having already thrown themselves together, having set no boundaries between each other, and being no longer able to differentiate, they no longer possess anything of their own. How can they on their own find the escape route that they have already blocked to that inner solitude?

They act from a source of mutual helplessness. If, with the best of intentions, they wish to avoid the convention that is approaching them (marriage, for example) they find themselves in the clutches of another conventional solution, one less obvious, but just as deadly. Everything surrounding them, spread wide about them, is — convention. There, where a dull mutuality, prematurely established, is the basis for living, *every* action is conventional. Every situation leading to such confusion has its convention, be it ever so unusual, that is, in the ordinary sense, immoral. Yes, even separation would be a conventional step, an impersonal, coincidental decision, a weak and fruitless decision. Whoever will seriously consider the question of love will find that, as with the question of death, difficult as it is, there is no enlightened answer, no solution, not the hint of a path has yet been found. And for these two deep concerns that we carry safely disguised within us and that we pass on unresolved, for them no comforting principle will be learned, none finding general agreement.

But to the same degree that we as individuals begin to explore life, to that degree shall these deep things surface for each of us in greater intimacy. The responsibility that the difficult work of love demands of our evolvement overwhelms us; it is larger than life. We, as yet beginners, are not equal to it. If we persevere after all, and take this love upon us, accepting it as a burden and a time of training, instead of losing ourselves to the frivolous and careless game behind which people have hidden themselves, not willing to face the most serious question of their being — then perhaps shall a small bit of progress be perceptible as well as some relief for those to come after us. That would be a great deal.

We are just now reaching the point where we can observe objectively and without judgment the relationship of one individual to a second one. Our attempts to live such a relationship are without a model. Yet, there already exists within our time frame some things intended to help our fainthearted beginner's steps. The girl and the woman in their own new unfolding will only temporarily be imitators of male incivilities, of men's ways, and repeaters of men's careers. After the insecurity of this transition has passed, it will be shown that women, through their wealth of (often ridiculous) disguises and many changes, have continued their quest only in order to purify their own beings of the distorting influences of the other sex. The women, within whom life dwells in a more direct, fruitful, and trusting way, must, after all, have become basically more mature, more human than the man. For he is easily pulled down by the weight of the lack of physical fruitfulness, pulled down under the surface of life; he professes to love that which he arrogantly and rashly underrates.

The simple humanity of woman, brought about through pain and abasement, shall then come to light when the convention of her ultra-feminism will have been stripped off, transforming her status in the world. The men, who today cannot yet feel it coming, shall be surprised and defeated by it. One day (in northern countries trustworthy signs can already be seen and heard), the girl and the woman shall exist with her name no longer contrasted to the masculine; it shall have a meaning in itself. It shall not bring to mind complement or limitation — only life and being: the feminine human being.

This progress shall transform the experience of love, presently full of error, opposed at first by men, who have been overtaken in their progress by women. It shall thoroughly change the love experience to the rebuilding of a relationship meant to be between two persons, no longer just between man and woman. And this more human love will be consummated, endlessly considerate and gentle, good and clear in its bonding and releasing; it shall resemble that love for which we must prepare painstakingly and with fervor, which will be comprised of two lonelinesses protecting one another, setting limits, and acknowledging one another.

And one more thing: Do not believe that this idea of a great love, which, when you were a boy was imposed upon you, has been lost. Can you not say that since then great and good wishes have ripened within you, and resolutions too, by which you live today? I believe that this idea of love remains so strong and mighty in your memory because it was your first deep experience of aloneness and the first inner work that you have done on your life.

faith

"It may be, as some extreme saints have implied,
that beneath the majesty of the infinite,
believers and non-believers are exactly alike."

—JOHN UPDIKE

Wouldn't Take Nothing for My Journey Now

MAYA ANGELOU

In 1903 the late Mrs. Annie Johnson of Arkansas found herself with two toddling sons, very little money, a slight ability to read and add simple numbers. To this picture add a disastrous marriage and the burdensome fact that Mrs. Johnson was a Negro.

When she told her husband, Mr. William Johnson, of her dissatisfaction with their marriage, he conceded that he too found it to be less than he expected, and had been secretly hoping to leave and study religion. He added that he thought God was calling him not only to preach but to do so in Enid, Oklahoma. He did not tell her that he knew a minister in Enid with whom he could study and who had a friendly, unmarried daughter. They parted amicably, Annie keeping the one-room house and William taking most of the cash to carry himself to Oklahoma.

Annie, over six feet tall, big-boned, decided that she would not go to work as a domestic and leave her "precious babes" to anyone else's care. There was no possibility of being hired at the town's cotton gin or lumber mill, but maybe there was a way to make the two factories work for her. In her words, "I looked up the road I was going and back the way I come, and since I wasn't satisfied, I decided to step off the road and cut me a new path." She told herself that she wasn't a fancy cook but that she could "mix groceries well enough to scare hungry away and from starving a man."

She made her plans meticulously and in secret. One early evening to see if she was ready, she placed stones in two-five gallon pails and carried them three miles to the cotton gin. She rested a little, and then, discarding some rocks, she walked in the darkness to the saw mill five miles farther along the dirt road. On her way back to her little house and her babies, she dumped the remaining rocks along the path.

That same night she worked into the early hours boiling chicken and frying ham. She made dough and filled the rolled-out pastry with meat. At last she went to sleep.

The next morning she left her house carrying the meat pies, lard, an iron brazier, and coals for a fire. Just before lunch she appeared in a empty lot behind the cotton gin. As the dinner noon bell rang, she dropped the savors into boiling fat and the aroma rose and floated over to the workers who spilled out of the gin, covered with white lint, looking like specters.

Most workers had brought their lunches of pinto beans and biscuits or crackers, onions and cans of sardines, but they were tempted by the hot meat pies which Annie ladled out of the fat. She wrapped them in newspapers, which soaked up the grease, and offered them for sale at a nickel each. Although business was slow, those first days Annie was determined. She balanced her appearances between the two hours of activity.

So, on Monday if she offered hot fresh pies at the cotton gin and sold the remaining cooled-down pies at the lumber mill for three cents, then on Tuesday she went first to the lumber mill presenting fresh, just-cooked pies as the lumbermen covered in sawdust emerged from the mill.

For the next few years, on balmy spring days, blistering summer noons, and cold, wet, and wintry middays, Annie never disappointed her customers, who could count on seeing the tall, brown-skin woman bent over her brazier, carefully turning the meat pies. When she felt certain that the workers had become dependent on her, she built a stall between the two hives of industry and let the men run to her for their lunchtime provisions.

She had indeed stepped from the road which seemed to have been chosen for her and cut herself a brand-new path. In years that stall became a store where customers could buy cheese, meal, syrup, cookies, candy, writing tablets, pickles, canned goods, fresh fruit, soft drinks, coal, oil, and leather soles for worn-out shoes.

Each of us has the right and responsibility to assess the roads which lie ahead, and those over which we have traveled, and if the future road looms ominously or unpromising, and the roads back uninviting, then we need to gather our resolve and, carrying only the necessary baggage, step off that road into another direction. If the new choice is also unpalatable, without embarrassment, we must be ready to change that as well.

The Book

ALAN WATTS

We do not need a new religion or a new bible. We need a new experience — a new feeling of what it is to be "I." The lowdown (which is, of course, the secret and profound view) on life is that our normal sensation of self is a hoax, or, at best, a temporary role that we are playing, or have been conned into playing — with our own tacit consent, just as every hypnotized person is basically willing to be hypnotized. The most strongly enforced of all known taboos is the taboo against knowing who or what you really are behind the mask of your apparently separate, independent, and isolated ego. I am not thinking of Freud's barbarous Id or Unconscious as the actual reality behind the façade of personality. Freud, as we shall see, was under the influence of a nineteenth-century fashion called "reductionism," a curious need to put down human culture and intelligence by calling it a fluky by-product of blind and irrational forces. They worked very hard, then, to prove that grapes can grown on thornbushes.

As is so often the way, what we have suppressed and overlooked is something startlingly obvious. The difficulty is that it is *so* obvious and basic that one can hardly find the words for it. The Germans call it a *Hintergedanke*, an apprehension lying tacitly in the back of our minds which we cannot easily admit, even to ourselves. The sensation of "I" as a lonely and isolated center of being is so powerful and commonsensical, and so fundamental to our modes of speech and thought, to our laws and social institutions, that we cannot experience selfhood except as something superficial in the scheme of the universe. I seem to be a brief light that flashes but once in all the aeons of time — a rare, complicated, and all-too-delicate organism on the fringe of biological evolution, where the wave of life bursts into individual, sparkling, and multicolored drops that gleam for a moment only to vanish forever. Under such conditioning it seems impossible and even absurd to realize that myself does not reside in the drop alone, but in the whole surge of energy which ranges from the galaxies to the nuclear fields in my body. At this level of existence "I" am immeasurably old; my forms are infinite and their comings and goings are simply the pulses or vibrations of a single and eternal flow of energy.

The difficulty in realizing this to be so is that conceptual thinking cannot grasp it. It is as if the eyes were trying to look at themselves directly, or as if one were trying to describe the color of a mirror in terms of colors reflected in the mirror. Just as sight is something more than all things seen, the foundation or "ground" of our existence and our awareness cannot be understood in terms of things that are known. We are forced, therefore, to speak of it through myth — that is, through special metaphors, analogies, and images which say what it is *like* as distinct from what it *is.* At one extreme of its meaning, "myth" is fable, falsehood, or superstition. But at another, "myth" is a useful and fruitful image by which we make sense of life in somewhat the same way that we can explain electrical forces by comparing them with the behavior of water or air. Yet "myth," in this second sense, is not to be taken literally, just as electricity is not to be confused with air or water. Thus in using myth one must take care not to confuse image with fact, which would be like climbing up the signpost instead of following the road.

For this reason The Book I would pass to my children would contain no sermons, no shoulds and oughts. Genuine love comes from knowledge, not from a sense of duty or guilt. How would you like to be an invalid mother with a daughter who can't marry because she feels she ought to look after you, and therefore hates you? My wish would be to tell, not how things ought to be, but how they are, and how and why we ignore them as they are. You cannot teach an ego to be anything but egotistic, even though egos have the subtlest ways of pretending to be reformed. The basic thing is therefore to dispel, by experiment and experience, the illusion of oneself as a separate ego. The consequences may not be behavior along the lines of *conventional* morality. It may well be as the squares said of Jesus, "Look at him! A glutton and a drinker, a friend of tax-gatherers and sinners!"

Furthermore, on seeing through the illusion of the ego, it is impossible to think of oneself as better than, or superior to, others for having done so. In every direction there is just the one Self playing its myriad games of hide-and-seek. Birds are not *better* than the eggs from which they have broken. Indeed, it could be said that a bird is one egg's way of becoming other eggs. Egg is ego, and bird is the liberated Self. There is a Hindu myth of the Self as a divine swan which laid the egg from which the world was hatched. Thus I am not even saying that you *ought* to break out of your shell. Sometime, somehow, you (the real you, the Self) will do it anyhow, but it is not impossible that the play of the Self will be to remain unawakened in most of its human disguises, and so bring the drama of life on earth to its close in a vast explosion. Another Hindu myth says that as time goes on, life in the world gets worse and worse, until at last the destructive aspect of the Self, the god Shiva, dances a terrible dance which consumes everything in fire. There follow, says the myth, 4,320,000 years of total peace during which the Self is just itself and does not play hide. And then the game begins again, starting off as a universe of perfect splendor which begins to deterio-rate only after 1,728,000 years, and every round of the game is so designed that the forces of darkness present themselves for only one third of the time, enjoying at the end a brief but quite illusory triumph.

Today we calculate the life of this planet alone in much vaster periods, but of all ancient civilizations the Hindus had the most imaginative vision of cosmic time. Yet remember, this story of the cycles of the world's appearance and disappear-ance is myth, not science, parable rather than prophecy. It is a way of illustrating the idea that the universe is *like* the game of hide-and-seek.

If, then, I am not saying that you *ought* to awaken from the ego-illusion and help save the world from disaster, why The Book? Why not sit back and let things take their course? Simply that it is part of "things taking their course" that I write. As a human being it is just my nature to enjoy and share philosophy. I do this in the same way that some birds are eagles and some doves, some flowers lilies and some roses. I realize, too, that the less I preach, the more likely I am to be heard.

The Dalai Lama

PATRICIA SMITH CHURCHLAND

A number of months ago, I, among a few other neuroscientists, was asked to give a tutorial on the brain to the Dalai Lama. We were told that he was simply very interested, that he wanted to know about the kinds of things we were working on, and he wanted to understand in order to think about things more wisely. So we had a meeting with him in Newport Beach.

Now, the profoundly interesting thing about the Dalai Lama was this: he had no dogma. He was willing to change his mind about anything depending on the nature of the evidence. He seemed to take as the most important aspect of the religion of Buddhism those questions of how to live a life. And there he talked about compassion, about honesty, and so forth. But he didn't advert to any dogmas about the nature of the universe: about whether the earth is in the center of the solar system, or about whether species were created, or whether there was a mind independent of the body, and so on. He said, "If those are the facts, those are the facts."

What I thought was important was that on the issues of science, issues of the nature of the universe, he wanted information from the people who knew, or the people who had the most information available. And he was not going to insist that the universe be one way because the Buddhists had thought it was so for two thousand years. He is deeply concerned with how people live their lives and with political issues of compassion, and it seemed to me this kind of separation of matters of fact on the one hand and matters of morals on the other hand was really quite important to him.

Be Still and Know

THICH NHAT HANH

Twenty years ago at a conference I attended of theologians and professors of religion, an Indian Christian friend told the assembly, "We are going to hear about the beauties of several traditions, but that does not mean that we are going to make a fruit salad." When it came my turn to speak, I said, "Fruit salad can be delicious! I have shared the Eucharist with Father Daniel Berrigan, and our worship became possible because of the sufferings we Vietnamese and Americans shared over many years." Some of the Buddhists present were shocked to hear I had participated in the Eucharist, and many Christians seemed truly horrified. To me, religious life is life. I do not see any reason to spend one's whole life tasting just one kind of fruit. We human beings can be nourished by the best values of many traditions.

Professor Hans Küng has said, "Until there is peace between religions, there can be no peace in the world." People kill and are killed because they cling too tightly to their own beliefs and ideologies. When we believe that ours is the only faith that contains the truth, violence and suffering will surely be the result. The second precept of the Order of Interbeing, founded within the Zen Buddhist tradition during the war in Vietnam, is about letting go of views: "Do not think the knowledge you presently possess is changeless, absolute truth. Avoid being narrow-minded and bound to present views. Learn and practice nonattachment from views in order to be open to receive others' viewpoints." To me, this is the most essential practice of peace.

Myths to Live By

JOSEPH CAMPBELL

And so, my friends, we don't know a thing, and not even our science can tell us sooth; for it is no more than, so to say, an eagerness for truths, no matter where their allure may lead. And so it seems to me that here again we have a still greater, more alive, revelation than anything our old religions ever gave to us or even so much as suggested. The old texts comfort us with horizons. They tell us that a loving, kind, and just father is out there, looking down upon us, ready to receive us, and ever with our own dear lives on his mind. According to our sciences, on the other hand, nobody knows *what* is out there, or if there is any "out there" at all. All that can be said is that there appears to be a prodigious display of phenomena, which our senses and their instruments translate to our minds according to the nature of our minds. And there is a display of a quite different kind of imagery from within, which we experience best at night, in sleep, but which may also break into our daylight lives and even destroy us with madness. What the background of these forms, external and internal, may be, we can only surmise and possibly move toward through hypotheses. What are they, or where, or why (to ask all the usual questions) is an absolute mystery — the only absolute known, because absolutely unknown; and this we must all now have the magnitude to concede.

There is no "Thou shalt!" any more. There is nothing one *has* to believe, and there is nothing one *has* to do. On the other hand, one can of course, if one prefers, still choose to play at the old Middle Ages game, or some Oriental game, or even some sort of primitive game. We are living in a difficult time, and whatever defends us from the madhouse can be applauded as good enough — for those without nerve.

When I was in India in the winter of 1954, in conversation with an Indian gentleman of just about my own age, he asked with a certain air of distance, after we had exchanged formalities, "What are you Western scholars now saying about the dating of the Vedas?"

The Vedas, you must know, are the counterparts for the Hindu of the Torah for the Jew. They are his scriptures of the most ancient date and therefore of the highest revelation.

"Well," I answered, "the dating of the Vedas has lately

been reduced and is being assigned, I believe, to something like, say, 1500 to 1000 B.C. As you probably know," I added, "there have been found in India itself the remains of an earlier civilization than the Vedic."

"Yes," said the Indian gentleman, not testily but firmly, with an air of untroubled assurance, "I know; but as an orthodox Hindu I cannot believe that there is anything in the universe earlier than the Vedas." And he meant that.

"Okay," said I. "Then why did you ask?"

To give old India, however, its due, let me conclude with the fragment of a Hindu myth that to me seems to have captured in a particularly apt image the whole sense of such a movement as we today are all facing at this critical juncture of our general human history. It tells of a time at the very start of the history of the universe when the gods and their chief enemies, the anti-gods, were engaged in one of their eternal wars. They decided this time to conclude a truce and in cooperation to churn the Milky Ocean — the Universal Sea — for its butter of immortality. They took for their churning-spindle the Cosmic Mountain (the Vedic counterpart of Dante's Mountain of Purgatory), and for a twirling-cord they wrapped the Cosmic Serpent around it. Then, with the gods all pulling at the head end and the anti-gods at the tail, they caused that Cosmic Mountain to whirl. And they had been churning thus for a thousand years when a great black cloud of absolutely poisonous smoke came up out of the waters, and the churning had to stop. They had broken through to an unprecedented source of power, and what they were experiencing first were its negative, lethal effects. If the work were to continue, some one of them was going to have to swallow and absorb that poisonous cloud, and, as all knew, there was but one who would be capable of such an act; namely, the archetypal god of yoga, Shiva, a frightening daemonic figure. He just took that entire poison cloud into his begging bowl and at one gulp drank it down, holding it by yoga at the leg of his throat, where it turned the whole throat blue; and he has been known as Blue Throat, Nilakantha, ever since. Then, when that wonderful deed had been accomplished, all the other gods and the anti-gods returned to their common labor. And they churned and they churned and they went right on tirelessly churning, until lo! a number of wonderful benefits began coming up out of the Cosmic Sea: the moon, the sun, an elephant with eight trunks came up, a glorious steed, certain medicines, and yes, at last! a great radiant vessel filled with the ambrosial butter.

This old Indian myth I offer as a parable for our world today, as an exhortation to press on with the work, beyond fear.

meditation

"We should invert our eyes and practice a sublime astronomy in the infinitude of our hearts . . . If we see the Milky Way, it is because it *actually exists in our souls*."

—JORGE LUIS BORGES

Silence

MOTHER TERESA

In the silence of the heart God speaks. If you face God in prayer and silence, God will speak to you. Then you will know that you are nothing. It is only when you realize your nothingness, your emptiness, that God can fill you with Himself. Souls of prayer are souls of great silence.

There is a very holy priest, who is also one of the best theologians in India right now. I know him very well, and I said to him, "Father, you talk all day about God. How close you must be to God!" And you know what he said to me? He said, "I may be talking much *about* God, but I may be talking very little *to* God." And then he explained, "I may be rattling off so many words and may be saying many good things, but deep down I do not have the time to listen. Because in the silence of the heart, God speaks."

We cannot put ourselves directly in the presence of God if we do not practice internal and external silence.

In silence we will find new energy and true unity. Silence gives us a new outlook on everything.

The essential thing is not what we say but what God says to us and through us. In that silence, He will listen to us; there He will speak to our soul, and there we will hear His voice.

Listen in silence because if your heart is full of other things you cannot hear the voice of God. But when you have listened to the voice of God in the stillness of your heart, then your heart is filled with God.

The contemplatives and ascetics of all ages and religions have sought God in the silence and solitude of the desert, forest, and mountains. Jesus himself spent forty days in the desert and the mountains, communing for long hours with the Father in the silence of the night.

We too are called to withdraw at certain intervals into deeper silence and aloneness with God, together as a community as well as personally. To be alone with him — not with our books, thoughts, and memories but completely stripped of everything — to dwell lovingly in his presence, silent, empty, expectant, and motionless. We cannot find God in noise or agitation.

In nature we find silence — the trees, flowers, and grass grow in silence. The stars, the moon, and the sun move in silence.

Silence of the heart is necessary so you can hear God

everywhere — in the closing of a door, in the person who needs you, in the birds that sing, in the flowers, in the animals.

What is essential is not what we say but what God tells us and what He tells others through us. In silence He listens to us; in silence He speaks to our souls. In silence we are granted the privilege of listening to His voice.

To make possible true inner silence, practice:

Silence of the eyes, by seeking always the beauty and goodness of God everywhere, closing them to the faults of others and to all that is sinful and disturbing to the soul;

Silence of the ears, by listening always to the voice of God and to the cry of the poor and the needy, closing them to all other voices that come from fallen human nature, such as gossip, tale-bearing, and uncharitable words;

Silence of the tongue, by praising God and speaking the life-giving Word of God that is the Truth, that enlightens and inspires, brings peace, hope, and joy, and by refraining from self-defense and every word that causes darkness, turmoil, pain, and death;

Silence of the mind, by opening it to the truth and knowledge of God in prayer and contemplation, like Mary who pondered the marvels of the Lord in her heart, and by closing it to all untruths, distractions, destructive thoughts, rash judgments, false suspicions of others, revengeful thoughts, and desires;

Silence of the heart, by loving God with our heart, soul, mind, and strength and one another as God loves, and avoiding all selfishness, hatred, envy, jealousy, and greed.

I shall keep the silence of my heart with greater care, so that in the silence of my heart I hear His words of comfort and from the fullness of my heart I comfort Jesus in the distressing disguise of the poor. For in the silence and purity of the heart God speaks.

January 1936

ALBERT CAMUS

Beyond the window there is a garden, but I can see only its walls. And a few branches flowing with light. A little higher, I see more branches, and higher still the sun. And of all the jubilation of the air that can be felt outdoors, of all that joy spread out over the world, I can see only shadows of branches playing on white curtains. There are also five rays of sunlight patiently pouring into the room the white scent of dried grass. A breeze, and the shadows on the curtains come to life. If a cloud covers up the sun and then lets it through again, the bright yellow of the vase of mimosa leaps out of the shade. The birth of this single flash of brightness is enough to fill me with a confused and whirling joy.

A prisoner in the cave, I lie alone and look at the shadow of the world. A January afternoon. But the heart of the air is full of cold. Everywhere a thin film of sunlight that you could split with a touch of your fingernail, but which clothes everything in an eternal smile. Who am I and what can I do — except enter into the movement of the branches and the light, be this ray of sunlight in which my cigarette smolders away, this soft and gentle passion breathing in the air? If I try to reach myself, it is at the heart of this light that I am to be found. And if I try to taste and understand this delicate flavor that contains the secret of the world, it is again myself that I find at the heart of the universe. Myself, that is to say this intense emotion which frees me from my surroundings. Soon, my attention will be filled again with other things and with the world of men. But let me cut out this moment from the cloth of time as other men leave a flower in the pages of a book. In it, they enclose the memory of a walk in which they were touched by love. I also walk through the world, but am caressed by a god. Life is short, and it is a sin to waste one's time. I waste my time all day long, while other people say that I do a great deal. Today is a resting place, and my heart goes out to meet itself.

If I still feel a grain of anxiety, it is at the thought of this unseizable moment slipping through my fingers like a ball of quicksilver. Let those who want to, stand aside from the world. I no longer feel sorry for myself, for now

I see myself being born. I am happy in this world for my kingdom is of this world. A cloud passes and a moment grows pale. I die to myself. The book opens at a well-loved page — how tasteless it is when compared to the book of the world. It is true that I have suffered, it is not true that I am suffering? And that I am drunk with this suffering because it is made up of that sun and these shadows, of this warmth and that coldness which can be felt afar off, at the very heart of the air? What cause to wonder if something dies or men suffer, when everything is written on this window where the sun pours forth its fullness? I can say, and in a moment I shall say, that what counts is to be true, and then everything fits in, both humanity and simplicity. And when am I truer and more transparent than when I *am* the world?

Moment of adorable silence. But the song of the world rises and I, a prisoner chained deep in the cave, am filled with delight before I have time to desire. Eternity is here while I was waiting for it. Now I can speak. I do not know what I could wish for rather than this continued presence of self with self. What I want now is not happiness but awareness. One thinks one has cut oneself off from the world, but it is enough to see an olive tree upright in the golden dust, or beaches glistening in the morning sun, to feel this separation melt away. Thus with me. I became aware of the possibilities for which I am responsible. Every minute of life carries with it its miraculous value, and its face of eternal youth.

New Mexico Letter

GEORGIA O'KEEFFE

TO ANITA POLLITZER

[CANYON, TEXAS] 11 SEPTEMBER 1916

Tonight I walked into the sunset — to mail some letters — the whole sky — and there is so much of it out here — was just blazing — and grey blue clouds were rioting all through the hotness of it — and the ugly little buildings and windmills looked great against it.

But some way or other I didn't seem to like the redness much so after I mailed the letters I walked home — and kept on walking —

The Eastern sky was all grey blue — bunches of clouds — different kinds of clouds — sticking around everywhere and the whole thing — lit up — first in one place — then in another with flashes of lightning —sometimes just sheet lightning — and sometimes sheet lightning with a sharp bright zigzag flashing across it—

I walked out past the last house — past the last locust —

tree — and sat on the fence for a long time — looking — just looking at the lightning — you see there was nothing but sky and flat prairie land — land that seems more like the ocean than anything else I know — There was a wonderful moon —

Well I just sat there and had a great time all by myself — Not even many night noises — just the wind —

I wondered what you are doing —

It is absurd the way I love this country — Then when I came back — it was funny — roads just shoot across blocks anywhere — all the houses looked alike — and I almost got lost — I had to laugh at myself — I couldn't tell which house was home —

I am loving the plains more than ever it seems — and the SKY — Anita you have never seen SKY — it is wonderful —

Overture

MARCEL PROUST

Many years had elapsed during which nothing of Combray, save what was comprised in the theatre and the drama of my going to bed there, had any existence for me, when one day in winter, as I came home, my mother, seeing that I was cold, offered me some tea, a thing I did not ordinarily take. I declined at first, and then, for no particular reason, changed my mind. She sent out for one of those short, plump little cakes called 'petites madeleines,' which look as though they had been moulded in the fluted scallop of a pilgrim's shell. And soon, mechanically, weary after a dull day with the prospect of a depressing morrow, I raised to my lips a spoonful of the tea in which I had soaked a morsel of the cake. No sooner had the warm liquid, and the crumbs with it, touched my palate than a shudder ran through my whole body, and I stopped, intent upon the extraordinary changes that were taking place. An exquisite pleasure had invaded my senses, but individual, detached, with no suggestion of its origin.

And at once the vicissitudes of life had become indifferent to me, its disasters innocuous, its brevity illusory — this new sensation having had on me the effect which love has of filling me with a precious essence; or rather this essence was not in me, it was myself. I had ceased now to feel mediocre, accidental, mortal. Whence could it have come to me, this all-powerful joy? I was conscious that it was connected with the taste of tea and cake, but that it infinitely transcended those savours, could not, indeed, be of the same nature as theirs. Whence did it come? What did it signify? How could I seize upon and define it?

I drink a second mouthful, in which I find nothing more than in the first, a third, which gives me rather less than the second. It is time to stop; the potion is losing its magic. It is plain that the object of my quest, the truth, lies not in the cup but in myself. The tea has called up in me, but does not itself understand, and can only repeat indefinitely with a gradual loss of strength, the same testimony; which I, too, cannot interpret, though I hope at least to be able to call upon the tea for it again and to find it there presently, intact and at my disposal, for my final enlightenment. I put down my cup and examine my own mind. It is for it to discover the truth. But how? What an abyss of uncertainty whenever the mind feels that some part of it has strayed beyond its own borders; when it, the seeker, is at once in the dark region through which it must go seeking, where all its equipment will avail if nothing. Seek? More than that: create. It is face to face with something which does not so far exist, to which it alone can give reality and substance, which it alone can bring into the light of day.

And I begin again to ask myself what it could have been, this unremembered state which brought with it no logical proof of its existence, but only the sense that it was a happy, that it was a real state in whose presence other states of consciousness melted and vanished. I decide to attempt to make it reappear. I retrace my thoughts to the moment at which I drank the first spoonful of tea. I find again the same state, illumined by no fresh light. I compel my mind to make one further effort, to follow and recapture once again the fleeting sensation. And that nothing may interrupt it in its course I shut out every obstacle, every extraneous idea, I stop my ears and inhibit all attention to the sounds which come from the next room. And then, feeling that my mind is growing fatigued without having any success to report, I compel it for a change to enjoy that distraction which I have just denied it, to think of other things, to rest and refresh itself before the supreme attempt. And then for the second time I clear an

empty space in front of it. I place in position before my mind's
eye the still recent taste of that first mouthful, and I feel something start within me, something that leaves its resting-place
and attempts to rise, something that has been embedded like an
anchor at a great depth; I do not know yet what it is, but I can
feel it mounting slowly; I can measure the resistance, I can
hear the echo of great spaces traversed.

Undoubtedly what is thus palpitating in the depths of my
being must be the image, the visual memory which, being
linked to the taste, has tried to follow it into my conscious
mind. But its struggles are too far off, too much confused;
scarcely can I perceive the colourless reflection in which are
blended the uncapturable whirling medley of radiant hues,
and I cannot distinguish its form, cannot invite it, as the one
possible interpreter, to translate to me the evidence of its con-
temporary, its inseparable paramour, the taste of cake soaked in
tea; cannot ask it to inform me what special circumstance is in
question, of what period in my past life.

Will it ultimately reach the clear surface of my consciousness, this memory, this old, dead moment which the magnet-
ism of an identical moment has travelled so far to importune,
to disturb, to raise up out of the very depths of my being? I
cannot tell. Now that I feel nothing, it has stopped, perhaps

gone down again into its darkness, from which who can say whether it will ever rise? Ten times over I must assay the task, must lean down over the abyss. And each time the natural laziness which deters us from every difficult enterprise, every work of importance, has urged me to leave the thing alone, to drink my tea and to think merely of the worries of to-day and of my hopes for to-morrow, which let themselves be pondered over without effort or distress of mind.

And suddenly the memory returns. The taste was that of the little crumb of madeleine which on Sunday mornings at Combray (because on those mornings I did not go out before church-time), when I went to say good day to her in her bed-room, my aunt Léonie used to give me, dipping it first in her cup of tea or of lime-flower tea. The sight of the little madeleine had recalled nothing to mind before I tasted it; perhaps because I had so often seen such things in the interval, without tasting them, on the trays in pastry-cook windows, that their image had dissociated itself from those Combray days to take its place among others more recent; perhaps because of those memories, so long abandoned and put out of mind, nothing now survived, everything was scattered; the forms of things, invading that of the little scallop-shell of pastry, so richly sensual under its severe, religious folds, were either obliterated or had been so long dormant as to have lost the power of expansion which would have allowed them to resume their place in my consciousness. But when from a long-distant past nothing subsists, after the people are dead, after the things are broken and scattered, still alone, more fragile, but with more vitality, more unsubstantial, more persistent, more faithful, the smell and taste of things remain poised a long time, like souls, ready to remind us, waiting and hoping for their moment; amid the ruins of all the rest; and bear unfaltering, in the tiny and almost impalpable drop of their essence, the vast structure of recollection.

And once I had recognized the taste of the crumb of madeleine soaked in her decoction of lime flowers which my aunt used to give me (although I did not yet know and must long postpone the discovery of why this memory made me so happy) immediately the old grey house upon the street where her room was, rose up like the scenery of a theatre to attach itself to the little pavilion, opening on to the garden, which had been built out behind it for my parents (the isolated pond which until that moment had been all that I could see), and with the house the town, from morning to night and in all weathers the Square where I was sent before luncheon, the streets along which I used to run errands, the country roads we took when it was fine. And just as the Japanese amuse themselves by filling a porcelain bowl with water and steeping in it little crumbs of paper which until then are without character or form, but, the moment they become wet, stretch themselves and bend, take on colour and distinctive shape, become flowers or houses or people, permanent and recognisable, so in that moment all the flowers in our garden and in M. Swann's park, and the water-lilies on the Vivonne and the good folk of the village and their little dwellings and the parish church and the whole of Combray and of its surroundings, taking their proper shapes and growing solid, sprang into being, town and gardens alike, from my cup of tea.

The Meaning of Life

ALBERT EINSTEIN

The most beautiful experience we can have is the mysterious. It is the fundamental emotion which stands at the cradle of true art and true science. Whoever does not know it and can no longer wonder, no longer marvel, is as good as dead, and his eyes are dimmed. It was the experience of mystery — even if mixed with fear — that engendered religion. A knowledge of the existence of something we cannot penetrate, our perceptions of the profoundest reason and the most radiant beauty, which only in their most primitive forms are accessible to our minds — it is this knowledge and this emotion that constitute true religiosity; in this sense, and in this alone, I am a deeply religious man. I cannot conceive of a God who rewards and punishes his creatures, or has a will of the kind that we experience in ourselves. Neither can I nor would I want to conceive of an individual that survives his physical death; let feeble souls, from fear or absurd egoism, cherish such thoughts. I am satisfied with the mystery of the eternity of life and with the awareness and a glimpse of the marvelous structure of the existing world, together with the devoted striving to comprehend a portion, be it ever so tiny, of the Reason that manifests itself in nature.

Moment of Wisdom

M . F . K .   F I S H E R

Tears do come occasionally into one's eyes, and they are more often than not a good thing. At least they are salty and, no matter what invisible wound they seep from, they purge and seal the tissues. But when they roll out and down the cheeks it is a different thing, and more amazing to one unaccustomed to such an outward and visible sign of an inward cleansing. Quick tears can sting and tease the eyeballs and their lids into suffusion and then a new clarity. The brimming and, perhaps fortunately, rarer kind, however, leaves things pale and thinned out, so that even a gross face takes on a porcelain-like quality, and — in my own case — there is a sensation of great fragility or weariness of the bones and spirit.

I have had the experience of such tears very few times. Perhaps it is a good idea to mention one or two of them, if for no other reason than to remind myself that such a pure moment may never come again.

When I was twelve years old, my family was slowly installing itself about a mile down Painter Avenue outside

Whittier, California, the thriving little Quaker town where I grew up, on an orange ranch with shaggy, neglected gardens and a long row of half-wild roses along the narrow county road. Our house sat far back in the tangle, with perhaps two hundred yards of gravel driveway leading in toward it.

There was a wide screened porch across the front of the house, looking into the tangle. It was the heart of the place. We sat there long into the cool evenings of summer, talking softly. Even in winter, we were there for lunch on bright days, and in the afternoon drinking tea or beer. In one corner, there was always a good pile of wood for the hearth fire in the living room, and four wide doors led into that room. They were open most of the time, although the fire burned day and night, brightly or merely a gentle token, all the decades we lived on the Ranch.

My grandmother had her own small apartment in the house, as seemed natural and part of the way to coexist, and wandering missionaries and other men of her own cut of cloth often came down the road to see her and discuss convocations and get money and other help. They left books of earnest import and dubious literary worth, like one printed in symbols for the young or illiterate, with Jehovah an eye surrounded by shooting beams of forked fire. Grandmother's friends, of whom I remember not a single one, usually stayed for a meal.

Mother was often absent from such unannounced confronta-
tions, prey to almost ritual attacks of what were referred to as
"sick headaches," but my father always carved at his seat,
head of the table. Grandmother, of course, was there. Father
left early, and we children went up to bed, conditioned to
complete lack of interest in the murmur of respectful manly
voices and our grandmother's clear-cut Victorian guidance of
the churchly talk below us. That was the pattern the first
months at the Ranch, before the old lady died, and I am sure
we ate amply and well, and with good manners, and we
accepted sober men in dusty black suits as part of being alive.

When we moved down Painter Avenue into what was
then real country, I was near intoxication from the flowers
growing everywhere — the scraggly roses lining the road, all
viciously thorned as they reverted to wildness, and poppies
and lupine in the ditches and still between the rows of orange
trees (soon to disappear as their seeds got plowed too deeply
into the profitable soil), and exotic bulbs springing up hit or
miss in our neglected gardens. I rooted around in all of it like a
virgin piglet snuffling for truffles. My mother gave me free
rein to keep the house filled with my own interpretations of
the word "posy." It was a fine season in life.

One day, I came inside, very dusty and hot, with a basket

of roses and weeds of beauty. The house seemed mine, airy and empty, full of shade. Perhaps everyone was in Whittier, marketing. I leaned my forehead against the screening of the front porch and breathed the wonderful dry air of temporary freedom, and off from the country road and onto our long narrow driveway came a small man, smaller than I, dressed in the crumpled hot black I recognized at once as the Cloth and carrying a small valise.

I wiped at my sweaty face and went to the screen door, to be polite to another of my grandmother's visitors. I wished I had stayed out, anywhere at all, being that age and so on, and aware of rebellion's new pricks.

He was indeed tiny, and frail in a way I had never noticed before in anyone. (I think this new awareness and what happened later came from the fact that I was alone in the family house and felt for the moment like a stranger made up of Grandmother and my parents and maybe God — that eye, Jehovah, but with no lightning.) He would not come in. I asked him if he would like some cool water, but he said no. His voice was thin. He asked to see Mother Holbrook, and when I told him she had died a few days before he did not seem at all bothered, and neither was I, except that he might be.

He asked if I would like to buy a Bible. I said no, we had many of them. His hands were too shaky and weak to open his satchel, but when I asked him again to come in, and started to open the door to go out to help him, he told me in such a firm way to leave him alone that I did. I did not reason about it, for it seemed to be an agreement between us.

He picked up his dusty satchel, saying goodbye in a very gentle voice, and walked back down the long driveway to the county road and then south, thinking God knows what hopeless thoughts. A little past our gate, he stopped to pick one of the dusty roses. I leaned my head against the screening of our porch and was astounded and mystified to feel slow fat quiet tears roll from my unblinking eyes and down my cheeks.

I could not believe it was happening. Where did they spring from, so fully formed, so unexpectedly? Where had they been waiting, all my long life as a child? What had just happened to me, to make me cry without volition, without a sound or a sob?

In a kind of justification of what I thought was a weakness, for I had been schooled to consider all tears as such, I thought, If I could have given him something of mine . . . If I were rich, I would buy him a new black suit . . . If I had next week's allowance and had not spent this week's on three

Cherry Flips. . . . If I could have given him some cool water or my love . . .

But the tiny old man, dry as a ditch weed, was past all that, as I came to learn long after my first passionate protest — past or beyond.

The first of such tears as mine that dusty day, which are perhaps rightly called the tears of new wisdom, are the most startling to one's supposed equanimity. Later, they have a different taste. Perhaps they seem more bitter because they are recognizable. But they are always as unpredictable. Once, I was lying with my head back, listening to a long program of radio music from New York, with Toscanini drawing fine blood music from his gang. I was hardly conscious of the sound — with my mind, anyway — and when it ended, my two ears, which I had never thought of as cup-like, were so full of silent tears that as I sat up they drenched and darkened my whole front with little gouts of brine. I felt amazed, beyond my embarrassment in a group of near-friends, for the music I had heard was not the kind I thought I liked, and the salty water had rolled down from my half-closed eyes like October rain, with no sting to it but perhaps promising a good winter.

Such things are, I repeat to myself, fortunately rare, for

they are too mysterious to accept with equanimity. I prefer not to dig too much into their comings, but it is sure that they cannot be evoked or foretold. If anger has a part in them, it is latent, indirect — not an incentive. The helpless weeping and sobbing and retching that sweeps over somebody who inadvertently hears Churchill's voice rallying Englishmen to protect their shores, or Roosevelt telling people not to be afraid of fear, or a civil-rights chieftain saying politely that there is such a thing as democracy — those violent physical reactions are proof of one's being alive and aware. But the slow, large tears that spill from the eye, flowing like unblown rain according to the laws of gravity and desolation — these are the real tears, I think. They are the ones that have been simmered, boiled, sieved, filtered past all anger and into the realm of acceptive serenity.

There is a story about a dog and an ape that came to love each other. The dog finally died, trying to keep the ape from returning to the jungle where he should have been all along and where none but another ape could follow. And one becomes the dog, the ape, no matter how clumsily the story is told. One is the hapless lover.

I am all of them. I feel again the hot dusty screening on my forehead as I watch the little man walk slowly out to the road and turn down past the ditches and stop for a moment by a scraggly rosebush. If I could only give him something, I think. If I could tell him something true.

It was a beginning for me, as the tears popped out so richly and ran down, without a sigh or cry. I could see clearly through them, with no blurring, and they did not sting. This last is perhaps the most astonishing and fearsome part, past denial of any such encounter with wisdom, or whatever it is.

death

"Perhaps being dead is passing into the ocean
of the waves that remain waves forever, so it is futile
to wait for the sea to become calm."

—ITALO CALVINO

Christmas 1992

ISABEL ALLENDE

Near dawn on Sunday, December 6, after a miraculous night in which the veils that conceal reality were parted, Paula died. It was at four in the morning. Her life ended without struggle, anxiety, or pain; in her passing there was only the absolute peace and love of those of us who were with her. She died in my arms, surrounded by her family, the thoughts of those absent, and the spirits of her ancestors who had come to her aid. She died with the same perfect grace that characterized all the acts of her life.

For some time, I had sensed the end. I knew with the same irrefutable certainty with which I awakened one morning in 1963 knowing that, only a few hours before, a daughter had been conceived in my womb. Death came with a light step. Paula's senses had been closing down, one by one, during the previous weeks; I think she could not hear any longer, her eyes were almost always closed, and she did not react when we touched or moved her. Inexorably, she was drifting away. I wrote a letter to my brother describing the symptoms imperceptible to others but evident to me, looking ahead with a strange mixture of anguish and relief. Juan answered with a single sentence: I am praying for her and for you. To lose Paula was unbearable torment, but it would be worse to watch her slowly agonize through the seven years foreseen by the I Ching sticks. That Saturday, Inés came early and we prepared the basins of water to bathe Paula and wash her hair; we set out her clothes for the day, and changed her sheets, as we did each morning. As we began to remove her nightgown, we noticed she was deep in an abnormal sopor, like a swoon, lifeless, and wearing the expression of a child, as if she has returned to the innocent age when she used to cut flowers in Granny's garden. I knew then that she was ready for her last adventure and, in one blessed instant, the confusion and terror of this year of affliction vanished, giving way to a diaphanous tranquillity. "Do you mind, Inés, I want to be alone with her," I asked. Inés threw herself on Paula and kissed her. "Take my sins with you, and try to find forgiveness for me up there," she pleaded, and she did not leave until I assured her that Paula had heard her and would serve as her messenger. I went to advise my mother, who hurriedly dressed and came down to Paula's room. The three of us were alone, accompanied by the cat, crouched in a corner with her inscrutable amber pupils fixed on the bed, waiting. Willie was doing the marketing and Celia and Nicolás never come on Saturdays, that's the day they clean their apartment, so I calculated we had several hours to say our farewells without interruptions. My daughter-in-law, however, woke that morning with a presentiment and, without a word of explanation, left her husband to the household chores, picked up her two children, and came to see us. She found my mother on one side of the bed and me on the other, silently caressing Paula. She says that the minute she entered the room, she noticed how still the air was, and what a delicate light enveloped us, and she realized that the moment we most feared and, at the same time, desired had come. She sat down with us while Alejandro played with his toy cars on the wheelchair and Andrea dozed on the rug, clutching her security blanket. A couple of hours later, Willie and Nicolás arrived; they, too, needed no explanation. They lighted a fire in the fireplace and put on Paula's favorite music: Mozart and Vivaldi concertos and Chopin nocturnes. We must call Ernesto, they decided, but his telephone in New York didn't answer and they concluded he was still on his return flight from China and could not be located. The petals from Willie's last roses were beginning to fall on the night table among the medicine bottles and syringes. Nicolás went out to buy flowers, and shortly after returned with armfuls of the flowers Paula had chosen for her wedding: the smell of tuberose and iris spread softly through the house while the hours, each slower than the last, became tangled in the clocks.

At midafternoon, Dr. Forrester came by and confirmed that something had changed in her patient's condition. She did not detect any fever or signs of pain, Paula's lungs were clear, and neither was this a new onslaught of porphyria, but the complex mechanism of her body was barely functioning. "It seems to be a cerebral hemorrhage," she said, and suggested calling a nurse to bring oxygen to the house, in view of the fact that we had agreed from the beginning we would never take her back to a hospital, but I vetoed that. There was no need to discuss it; everyone in the family had concurred that we would not prolong her agony, only make her comfortable. Unobtrusively, the doctor sat down near the fireplace to wait, she, too, caught up in the magic of that unique time. She would spend all night with us, not as a physician, but as the friend she had become. How simple life is, when all is said and done. . . . In this year of torment, I had gradually been letting go: first I said goodbye to Paula's intelligence, then to her vitality and her company, now, finally, I had to part with her body. I had lost everything, and my daughter was leaving me, but the one essential thing remained: love. In the end, all I have left is the love I give her.

I watched the sky grow dark beyond the large windows. At that hour, the view from the hill where we live is extraordinary; the water of the Bay is like phosphorescent steel as the landscape turns to a fresco of shadows and lights. As night approached, the exhausted children fell asleep on the floor, covered with a blanket, and Willie busied himself in the kitchen preparing something to eat; we had only recently realized that none of us had eaten all day. He came back after a while with a tray and a bottle of champagne we had saved all year for the moment when Paula waked again in this world. I couldn't eat, but I toasted my daughter so she would awake happy in another life. We lighted candles, and Celia picked up her guitar and sang Paula's songs; she has a deep warm voice that seems to issue from the earth itself, and her sister-in-law loved to hear her. "Sing just for me," she would coax Celia, "sing low." A wondrous lucidity allowed me to live those hours fully, with penetrating intuition and all five senses alert, as well as others whose existence I hadn't been aware of. The warm glow of the candles illuminated my daughter—

silken skin, crystal bones, the shadows of her eyelashes —
now sleeping forever. Transported by the intensity of our feeling for Paula, and the loving comradeship women share during the fundamental rituals of life, my mother, Celia, and I
improvised the last ceremonies: we sponged Paula's body,
anointed her skin with cologne, dressed her in warm clothing
so she wouldn't feel cold, put the rabbit fur slippers on her
feet, and combed her hair. Celia placed photographs of
Alejandro and Andrea in her hands: "Look out for them,"
she asked. I wrote our names on a piece of paper, brought my
grandmother's bridal orange blossoms and one of Granny's silver teaspoons, and placed all of them on Paula's breast for her
to take as a remembrance, along with my grandmother's silver
mirror, because I reasoned that if it had protected me for fifty
years, surely it would safeguard Paula during that last cross-
ing. Now Paula was opal, alabaster, translucent . . . and so
cold! The cold of death comes from within, like a blazing,
internal bonfire; when I kissed her, ice lingered on my lips
like a burn. Gathered around her bed, we looked through old
photographs and remembered the happiest times of the past,
from the first dream in which Paula revealed herself to me,
long before she was born, to her comic fit of jealousy when
Celia and Nicolás were married. We celebrated the gifts she

had given us in life, and all of us said goodbye and prayed in our own way. As the hours went by, something solemn and sacred filled the room, just as on the occasion of Andrea's birth. The two moments are much alike: birth and death are made of the same fabric. The air became more and more still; we moved slowly, in order not to disturb our hearts' repose. We were filled with Paula's spirit, as if we were all one being and there was no separation among us: life and death were joined. For a few hours, we experienced that reality the soul knows, absent time or space.

I slipped into bed beside my daughter, cradling her against my bosom, as I had when she was young. Celia removed the cat, and arranged the two sleeping children so their bodies would warm their aunt's feet. Nicolás took his sister's hand; Willie and my mother sat on either side, surrounded by ethereal beings, by murmurs and tenuous fragrances from the past, by ghosts and apparitions, by friends and relatives, living and dead. All during the slow night, we waited, remembering the difficult moments, but especially the happy ones, telling stories, crying a little and smiling a lot, honoring the light of Paula as she sank deeper and deeper into the final sleep, her breast barely rising at slower and slower intervals. Her mission in this world was to unite all those who passed through her life, and that night we all felt sheltered beneath her starry wings, immersed in that pure silence where perhaps angels reign. Voices became murmurs, the shape of objects and the faces of our family began to fade, silhouettes fused and blended; suddenly I realized that others were among us. Granny was there in her percale dress and marmalade-stained apron, with her fresh scent of plums and large blue eyes. Tata, with his Basque beret and rustic cane was sitting in a chair near the bed. Beside him, I saw a small, slender woman with Gypsy features, who smiled at me when our glances met: Memé, I suppose, but I didn't dare speak to her for fear she would shimmer and vanish like a mirage. In other corners of the room, I thought I saw Mama Hilda with her knitting in her hands, my brother Juan, praying beside the nuns and children from Paula's school in Madrid, my father-in-law, still young, and a court of kindly old people from the geriatric home Paula used to visit in her childhood. Only a while later, the unmistakable hand of Tío Ramón fell on my shoulder, and I clearly heard Michael's voice; to my right, I saw Ildemaro, looking at Paula with the tenderness he reserved just for her. I felt Ernesto's presence materializing through the window-pane; he was barefoot, dressed in aikido attire, a solid figure that crossed the room without touching the floor and leaned over the bed to kiss his wife on the lips. "Soon, my beautiful girl; wait for me on the other side," he said, and removed the cross he always wore and placed it around her neck. Then I handed him the wedding ring I had worn for exactly one year, and he slipped it on Paula's finger, as he had the day they were married. Then I was again in the portentous dream I had in Spain, in the silo-shaped tower filled with doves, but now my daughter wasn't twelve, she was twenty-eight years young; she was not wearing her checked overcoat but a white tunic, and her hair was not pulled back into a ponytail but hanging loose to her shoulders. She began to rise, and I with her, clinging to the cloth of her dress. Again I heard Memé's voice: *No one can go with her, she has drunk the potion of death. . . .* But I pushed upward with my last strength and grasped her hand, determined not to let go, and when we reached the top of the tower I saw the roof open and we ascended together. Outside, it was already dawn; the sky was streaked with gold and the countryside beneath our feet gleamed, washed by a recent rain. We flew over valleys and hills, and finally descended into a forest of ancient redwoods, where a breeze rustled among the branches and a bold bird defied winter with its solitary song. Paula pointed to the stream; I saw fresh roses lying along its banks and a white powder of calcined bones on the bottom, and I heard the music of thousands of voices whispering among the trees. I felt myself sinking into that cool water, and knew that the voyage through pain was ending in an absolute void. As I dissolved, I had the revelation that the void was filled with everything the universe holds. Nothing and everything, at once. Sacramental light and unfathomable darkness. I am the void, I am everything that exists, I am in every leaf of the forest, in every drop of the dew, in every particle of ash carried by the stream, I am Paula and I am also Isabel, I am nothing and all other things in this life and other lives, immortal.

Godspeed, Paula, woman.

Welcome, Paula, spirit.

Letters to My Son

KENT NERBURN

Once many years ago I was present at a total eclipse of the sun. I had climbed to the top of a high hill and had sat down to wait. It was early morning, slightly past sunup. Birds were singing in the trees around me. Far below on a hillside cows were grazing and horses rustled in the tall grasses.

When the moment came the sun began to darken. The horses were silent, the cows stood still. The birds ceased their chirping. As the sun disappeared behind the moon, the earth became still. The cows sank to their knees and the birds placed their heads beneath their wings.

Only the ghostly corona of the hidden sun remained to cast a fragile light on the enveloping darkness. There was no wind. There was no sound. The light of the sun had been taken from us and the world was cast into a great darkness.

At that moment something momentous happened: I no longer feared death. I felt annihilation, but annihilation into a oneness. I thought of my uncle who at that moment lay dying thousands of miles away. I thought of his fear and his loneliness and wished for all the world that he could have been with me for those seconds when the sun gave up its light.

I can't put a name to the knowledge I gained. It was too far beyond the human for me to understand. But I know it had to do with death, and I know it had to do with the great darkness into which we all must go.

There was a peace there, a peace that surpasses all understanding.

When fears of death overwhelm me, as they do at moments of sickness or great danger, I think of that hilltop and the birds with their heads tucked beneath their wings. All of us — me, the birds, the cows, and the horses — had been taken up into something larger than life itself.

Our selves had been obliterated; our individuality taken from us. Yet there was no impulse to scream against that obliteration. We were subsumed into something so great that we accepted it like the tranquil embrace of a long-sought sleep.

If that moment on the hillside contained truth — and I think it did — we do death no justice by measuring it against ourselves. We are too small; it is too great. What we fear is only the loss of the self, and the self knows eternity like a shadow knows the sun.

So, fear dying if you must. It takes from us the only life that we can understand, and that is a worthy loss to mourn. But do not fear death. It is something too great to celebrate, too great to fear. Either it brings us to a judgment, so it is ours to control by the kind of life we live, or it annihilates us into the great rhythm of nature, and we join the eternal peace of the revolving heavens.

In either case, I believe in my heart that it is ours to trust.

In the brief moment when I stood on that hillside while the earth's light went out, I felt no indifference and no sense of loss. Instead I felt an unutterable sense of gain, a shattering of all my own boundaries into a vast sense of peace.

If that was a moment of death, death should hold no terror, and we should embrace our dying as a momentary passage into the great harmony of eternity.

Perhaps we cannot hear that harmony now. Perhaps we even hear it as a vast and empty silence. But we should not be deceived. That vastness is not empty, it is a presence. Even in the greatest places the silence has a sound.

Gift from the Sea

ANNE MORROW LINDBERGH

I pick up my sisal bag. The sand slips softly under my feet. The time for reflection is almost over.

The search for outward simplicity, for inner integrity, for fuller relationship — is this not a limited outlook? Of course it is, in one sense. Today a kind of planetal point of view has burst upon mankind. The world is rumbling and erupting in ever-widening circles around us. The tensions, conflicts and sufferings even in the outermost circle touch us all, reverberate in all of us. We cannot avoid these vibrations.

But just how far can we implement this planetal awareness? We are asked today to feel compassionately for everyone in the world; to digest intellectually all the information spread out in public print; and to implement in action every ethical impulse aroused by our hearts and minds. The interrelatedness of the world links us constantly with more people than our hearts can hold. Or rather — for I believe the heart is infinite — modern communication loads us with more problems than the human frame can carry. It is good, I think, for our hearts, our minds, our imaginations to be stretched; but body, nerve, endurance and life-span are not as elastic. My life cannot implement in action the demands of all the people to whom my heart responds. I cannot marry all of them, or bear them all as children, or care for them all as I would my parents in illness or old age. Our grandmothers, and even — with some scrambling — our mothers, lived in a circle small enough to let them implement in action most of the impulses of their hearts and minds. We were brought up in a tradition that has now become impossible, for we have extended our circle throughout space and time.

Faced with this dilemma what can we do? How can we adjust our planetary awareness to our Puritan conscience? We are forced to make some compromise. Because we cannot deal with the many as individuals, we sometimes try to simplify the many into an abstraction called the mass. Because we cannot deal with the complexity of the present, we often override it and live in a simplified dream of the future. Because we cannot solve our own problems right here at home, we talk about problems out there in the world. An escape process goes on from the intolerable burden we have placed upon ourselves. But can one really feel deeply for an abstraction called the mass? Can one make the future a substitute for the present? And what guarantee have we that the future will be any better if we neglect the present? Can one solve world problems when one is unable to solve one's own? Where have we arrived in this process? Have we been successful, working at the periphery of the circle and not at the center?

If we stop to think about it, are not the real casualties in modern life just these centers I have been discussing: the here, the now, the individual and his relationships. The present is passed over in the race for the future; the here is neglected in favor of the there; and the individual is dwarfed by the enormity of the mass. America, which has the most glorious present still existing in the world today, hardly stops to enjoy it, in her insatiable appetite for the future. Perhaps the historian or the sociologist or the philosopher would say that we are still propelled by our frontier energy, still conditioned by our pioneer pressures or our Puritan anxiety to "do ye next thing." Europe, on the other hand, which we think of as being enamored of the past, has since the last war, strangely enough, been forced into a new appreciation of the present. The good past is so far away and the near past is so horrible and the future is so perilous, that the present has a chance to expand into a golden eternity of here and now. Europeans today are enjoying the moment even if it means merely a walk in the country on Sunday or sipping a cup of black coffee at a sidewalk café.

Perhaps we never appreciate the here and now until it is challenged, as it is beginning to be today even in America. And have we not also been awakened to a new sense of the dignity of the individual because of the threats and temptations to him, in our time, to surrender his individuality to the mass — whether it be industry or war or standardization of thought and action? We are now ready for a true appreciation of the value of the here and the now and the individual.

The here, the now, and the individual, have always been the special concern of the saint, the artist, the poet, and — from time immemorial — the woman. In the small circle of the home she has never quite forgotten the particular uniqueness of each member of the family; the spontaneity of now; the vividness of here. This is the basic substance of life. These are the individual elements that form the bigger entities like mass, future, world. We may neglect these elements, but we cannot dispense with them. They are the drops that make up the stream. They are the essence of life itself. It may be our special function to emphasize again these neglected realities, not as a retreat from greater responsibilities but as a first real step toward a deeper understanding and solution of them. When we start at the center of ourselves, we discover something worthwhile extending toward the periphery of the circle. We find again some of the joy in the now, some of the peace in the here, some of the love in me and thee which go to make up the kingdom of heaven on earth.

The waves echo behind me. Patience — Faith — Openness, is what the sea has to teach. Simplicity — Solitude — Intermittency. . . . But there are other beaches to explore. There are more shells to find. This is only a beginning.

Autumn

GRETEL EHRLICH

Autumn teaches us that fruition is also death; that ripeness is a form of decay. The willows, having stood for so long near water, begin to rust. Leaves are verbs that conjugate the seasons.

Today the sky is a wafer. Placed on my tongue, it is a wholeness that has already disintegrated; placed under the tongue, it makes my heart beat strongly enough to stretch myself over the winter brilliances to come. Now I feel the tenderness to which this season rots. Its defenselessness can no longer be corrupted. Death is its purity, its sweet mud. The string of storms that came across Wyoming like elephants tied tail to trunk falters now and bleeds into a stillness.

There is neither sun, nor wind, nor snow falling. The hunters are gone; snow geese waddle in grainfields. Already, the elk have started moving out of the mountains toward sheltered feed-grounds. Their great antlers will soon fall off like chandeliers shaken from ballroom ceilings. With them the light of these autumn days, bathed in what Tennyson called "a mockery of sunshine," will go completely out.

About the Authors

Among **DIANE ACKERMAN**'s well-known writings are *A Natural History of the Senses*, *A Natural History of Love*, and *The Moon by Whale Light*. She has received grants from the National Endowment for the Arts and The Rockefeller Foundation.

ISABEL ALLENDE, noted author of *The House of the Spirits* and *Eva Luna*, began writing *Paula* "in an irrational attempt to overcome terror" when she discovered her daughter had slipped into a coma. What emerges is a healing autobiographical story.

Born in 1928, **MAYA ANGELOU**'s life is chronicled in her four autobiographical works, which begin with *I Know Why the Caged Bird Sings*. While her books attest to difficult life experiences, they highlight her spirit of growth in the face of hardship.

JOSEPH CAMPBELL's interest in myth germinated with his early boyhood fascination with Native American cultures. Campbell's most important works are *The Hero with a Thousand Faces* and *The Masks of God* series.

The Algerian-born French writer **ALBERT CAMUS** is best-known for his works *The Stranger* and *The Myth of Sisyphus*. Camus's work often fell into the realm of the "absurd," the failure of humans to comprehend their condition.

While practicing Western medicine, **DEEPAK CHOPRA** began to study *Ayurveda*, the ancient Indian science of healing that treats the body and mind as one system. He has written many books, including *Ageless Body, Timeless Mind*.

PATRICIA SMITH CHURCHLAND is a professor of philosophy at the University of California. She explores the ways in which neuroscience can inform philosophical questions of consciousness and personal choice.

GRETEL EHRLICH has spent her life working on ranches and writing from the mountains of Wyoming. Before writing, she worked as a documentary filmmaker.

Most famous for the theory of relativity, **ALBERT EINSTEIN** won the Nobel Prize for physics in 1921. Outside the world of physics, Einstein worked, wrote, and spoke extensively for freedom, democracy, and peace.

Born in Michigan in 1908, **M.F.K. FISHER** spent her adult life living in California, France, and Switzerland, where she was a vineyardist. She has written numerous books on gastronomy, as well as novels and poetry.

Before being appointed secretary-general for the United Nations from 1953 until 1961, **DAG HAMMARSKJÖLD** played an important part in shaping Sweden's policy, yet never joined any political party. *Markings* was his private journal.

Born in Eatonville, Florida, in 1891, **ZORA NEALE HURSTON** published *Dust Tracks on a Road*, an autobiographical account, in 1942. Her works include *Mules and Men* and *Their Eyes Were Watching God*.

The diary of **FRIDA KAHLO** provides a dizzying journey into the intimate inner life of this legendary Mexican artist, who began painting from her bed after suffering a severe bus accident at age eighteen.

In our multicultural society, **MARTIN LUTHER KING, JR.**'s dream of a community built on equality is as timely today as it was thirty years ago, when the Civil Rights leader led the U.S. to desegregation through nonviolent resistance.

Rabbi **HAROLD KUSHNER** was ordained in 1960 and served 24 years at the Temple Israel. His *When Bad Things Happen to Good People* (1981) was named one of the ten most influential books in recent history by the Book-of-the-Month Club.

In *Gift from the Sea* (1955), **ANNE MORROW LINDBERGH** explores the married woman's struggle for identity from the perspective of a woman at the seashore. Married to pilot Charles, she was the first woman to obtain a glider pilot's license.

In *The Wisdom of the Desert*, **THOMAS MERTON** brought together the sayings of the hermetic Desert Fathers. Merton also chose the solitary life of a Trappist Monk but shared his path through more than fifty works.

In 1950 **MOTHER TERESA** started The Missionaries of the Charity, dedicated to "service to the poorest of the poor." While her work has been seen as helping the masses, she gave her love to individuals. As she put it, her way was "just one, one, one."

KENT NERBURN's *Letters to My Son* offers guidance on core human issues such as love, work, and death. Highly involved with Native Americans, Nerburn developed the Red Lake Ojibwe Reservation oral history project in Minnesota, where he lives.

The book *Living Buddha, Living Christ* brings together several of the essential concepts of Buddhist monk **THICH NHAT HANH**: tolerance, dialogue, and the practice of God. The exiled Vietnamese monk lives in France.

In 1924 **GEORGIA O'KEEFFE** first painted the voluptuous flowers that became her signature. In 1946 the stark New Mexico desert became her permanent home. O'Keeffe was the first woman to be given a retrospective at the Museum of Modern Art.

WALKER PERCY's first novel, *The Moviegoer* (1961), won the National Book Award. Through humor, compassion, and colorful characters, Percy explores the individual's struggle to find faith and connection in an absurd world.

French novelist **MARCEL PROUST** is best known for his life-work, *Remembrance of Things Past*, which he began in 1908 and continued until he died in 1922. In this book, Proust's writing becomes a vehicle for introspection and self-analysis.

Known as the greatest German poet of the 20th Century, **RAINER MARIA RILKE** is best known for *The Duino Elegies*. His late writing is characterized by highly nuanced images and novel manipulation of the German language.

Philosopher **ALAN WATTS** is known for his original interpretations of Zen Buddhism. His advice, "Don't look for the creation of the universe at some distance point in time behind us; it is now in the present," reminds us that what we do is what becomes; the world is dynamic, not static.

Acknowledgments

Ackerman excerpt from A NATURAL HISTORY OF LOVE by Diane Ackerman. ©1994 by Diane Ackerman. Reprinted by permission of Vintage Books, a division of Random House, Inc.

Allende excerpt from EPILOGUE from PAULA by Isabel Allende. Translation ©1995 by HarperCollins Publishers. Reprinted by permission of Harper-Collins Publishers, Inc.

Angelou excerpt from WOULDN'T TAKE NOTHING FOR MY JOURNEY NOW by Maya Angelou. ©1993 by Maya Angelou. Reprinted by permission of Random House, Inc.

Campbell excerpt from "The Impact of Science on Myth," from MYTHS TO LIVE BY by Joseph Campbell. ©1972 by Joseph Campbell. Used by permission of Viking Penguin, a division of Penguin Books USA, Inc.

Camus excerpt from NOTEBOOKS 1935-1942 by Albert Camus, trans., Philip Thody. ©1963 by Hamish Hamilton Ltd. and Alfred A. Knopf, Inc. Reprinted by permission of Alfred A. Knopf, Inc.

Chopra excerpt from AGELESS BODY, TIMELESS MIND by Deepak Chopra. ©1993 by Deepak Chopra, M.D. Reprinted by permission of Harmony Books, a division of Crown Publishers, Inc.

Churchland excerpt from BILL MOYERS, A WORLD OF IDEAS II: PUBLIC OPINIONS FROM PRIVATE CITIZENS edited by Andie Tucher. ©1990 by Public Affairs Television, Inc. Reprinted by permission of Doubleday, a division of The Bantam Doubleday Dell Publishing Group, Inc.

Ehrlich excerpt from THE SOLACE OF OPEN SPACES by Gretel Ehrlich. ©1985 by Gretel Ehrlich. Used by permission of Viking Penguin, a division of Penguin Books USA Inc.

Mother Teresa excerpt from NO GREATER LOVE by Mother Teresa ©1996 by New World Library. Reprinted with permission of New World Library, Novato, CA.

Nerburn passage excerpted from LETTERS TO MY SON by Kent Nerburn ©1994 by Kent Nerburn. Reprinted by permission of New World Library, Novato, CA.

Nhat Hanh excerpt reprinted by permission of Riverhead Books, a Division of The Putnam Publishing Group from LIVING BUDDHA, LIVING CHRIST by Thich Nhat Hanh. ©1995 by Thich Nhat Hanh.

O'Keeffe letter from GEORGIA O' KEEFFE ART AND LETTERS. ©1987 by the Estate of Georgia O'Keeffe. Reprinted by permission The Georgia O'Keeffe Foundation, Abiquiu, New Mexico.

Percy excerpt from THE MOVIEGOER by Walker Percy. ©1960, 1961 by Walker Percy. Reprinted by permission of Alfred A. Knopf, Inc.

Proust excerpt from REMEMBRANCE OF THINGS PAST by Marcel Proust, trans. by C.K. Scott Moncrieff & Terence Kilmartin. Translation ©1981 by Random House, Inc. and Chatto & Windus. Reprinted by permission of Random House, Inc.

Rilke passage excerpted from LETTERS TO A YOUNG POET by Rainer Maria Rilke, trans., Burnham. ©1992 by New World Library. Reprinted by permission of New World Library, Novato, CA.

Watts excerpt from THE BOOK by Alan Watts. ©1966 by Alan Watts. Reprinted by permission of Pantheon Books, a division of Random House, Inc.